For Alan Turing,
● year old me,
and anyone who cannot answer 8 X 3

MULTIC●LOUR MATHS CALCULATE IN COLOUR

This book belongs to

First printing edition 2024

www.multicolourmaths.com
www.brooktate.com

Dear future Mathemartician,

My name is Brook. I'm an artist. I paint people, cartoons, puppets, and sometimes I even paint my own face and turn into a zebra. For as long as I can remember I have loved to paint. The one thing I have **not** loved is…maths.

But…

Whilst scribbling in my sketchbook I discovered a way to **paint** it, and now I **LOVE** maths. I thought it might be fun, and maybe even helpful to share what I've discovered.

So get ready for a maths lesson like no other…

Crayons out.

Colours bright.

Let's calculate in COLOUR!

It was the last day of December 2023 and I was sat under a tree in India *trying* to get better at maths. But there was one main problem…I didn't like looking at numbers.

So I painted a colour chart in my sketchbook and counted how many *main* colours there are…

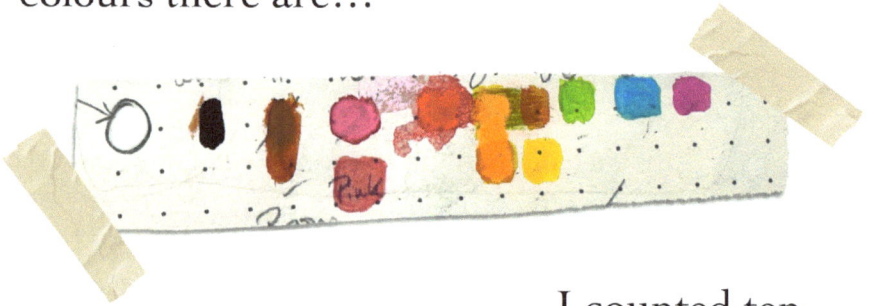

…I counted ten.

How many digits do we have?

Ten.

I'd found my new numbers…

A circle of colour is a number.
Not growing. Not shrinking.
Just a number, happy as it is.

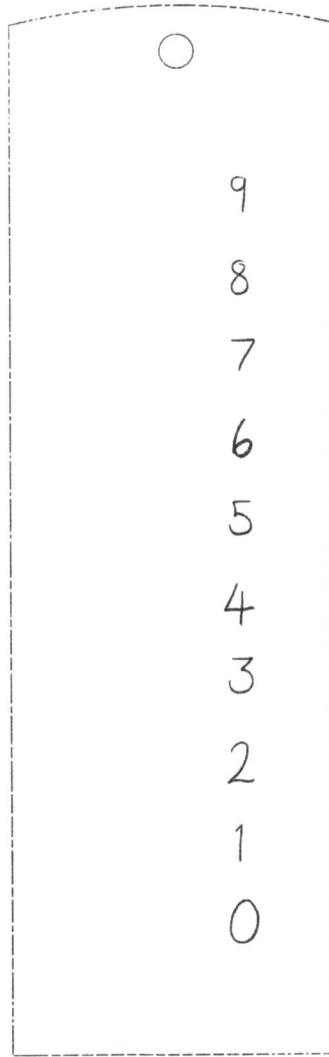

9   9

8   8

7   7

6   6

5   5

4   4

3   3

2   2

1   1

0   0

You might find a bookmark helpful…

Addition and Subtraction

We'll start simply.

$$1 + 2$$

And we'll calculate from the bottom up…

What colour
will this
circle be?

+ 2

1

Let's add some more…

$$3 + 5$$

what colour
will this
circle be?

+ 5

3

+ 2

1

Now let's read it from top to bottom.
You can even turn the book upside down…

The teardrop balloon shape represents
addition **and** subtraction! It just depends
on what direction you read it!

You can read a calculation in any direction.
Have a go at completing these…

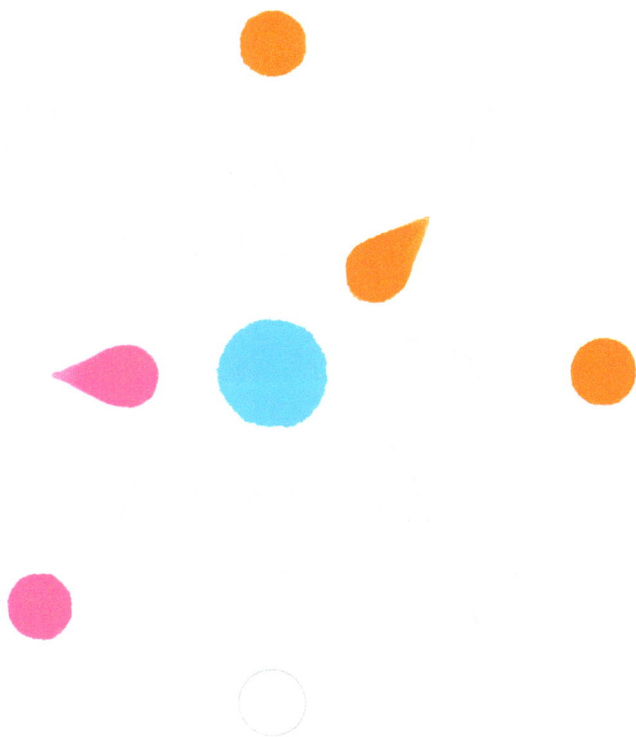

Hmmm…what will ten look like?

Well, ten is represented with 1 and 0.

0 is white

1 is black

So…

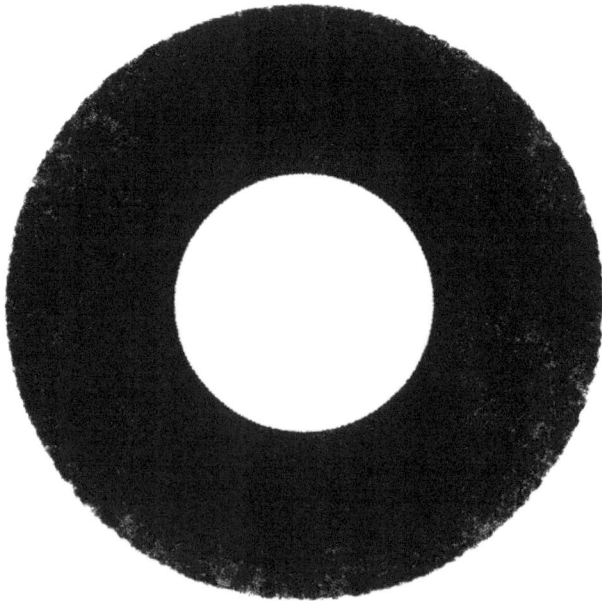

…is ten.

If ten is black around white,
what is missing from this picture…

If this is 18

and this is 81

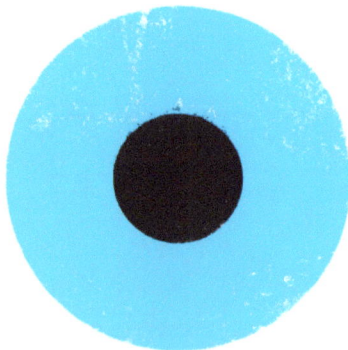

...what are these?

I used to struggle knowing the answers to simple sums off the top of my head. But now I can see them in my minds eye and it really helps me.

Here are some common combinations as colour calculations…

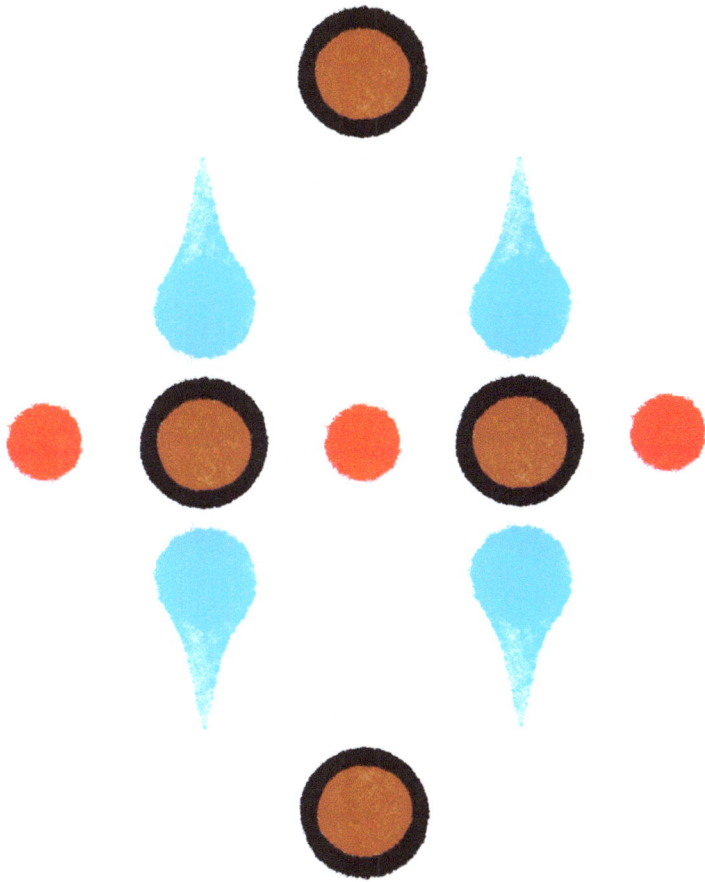

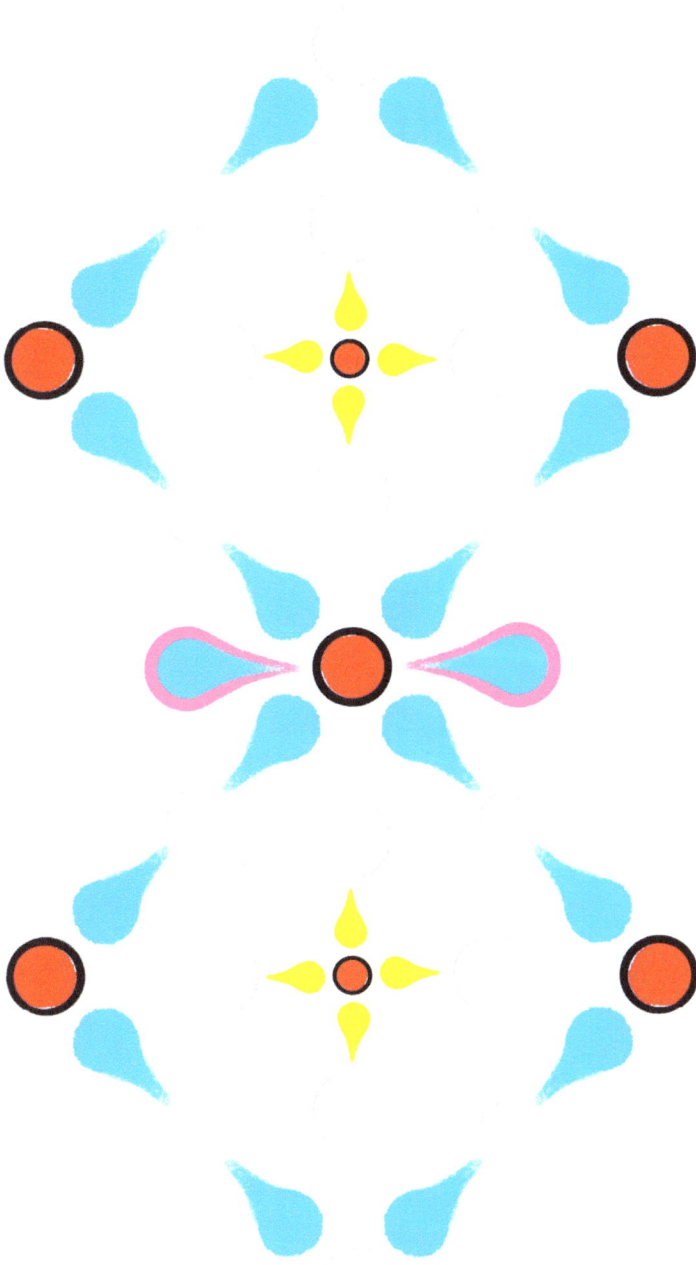

Multiplication and Division

Oooo…another shape

When I was ● years old I started learning my times tables at school. I found it very, *very* difficult. I just couldn't get them to stick in my brain.

But pictures stick in my brain whether I want them to or not. Our brains are very good at remembering pictures and patterns, and this is why colours have *really* helped me with learning the times tables…

Let's get to it…

3 x 2

x2    or...

The same mirroring magic happens here too.

A triangle represents multiply **and** divide.

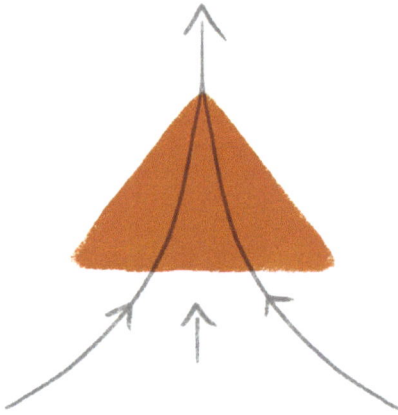

Multiply

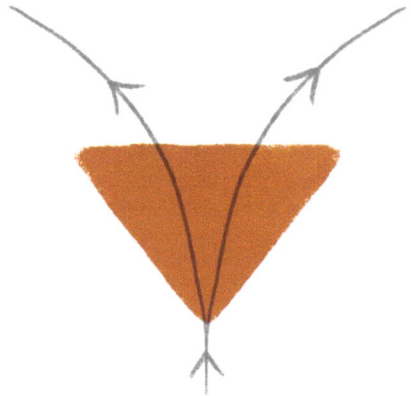

Divide

I imagine it working like this...

Now you know the three main shapes to calculate in colour. Let's create some artwork that might help you remember some tricky times tables…

Apparently this is one of the times tables people forget the most…

Paint or draw your own version on each side, then close the book and try recreating it on a blank piece of paper.

Can you remember it?

I've designed a bunch of patterns on the next few pages which might help you remember some more times tables.

You can complete them in the book and then create your own versions on seperate paper or material. You could even cut the pages out and send them to a friend!

Swirl away...

I hope you're enjoying this so far! Have a go at creating your own pictures from scratch and see what different styles you can find. The patterns in this book are just prompts that I hope will help you get the hang of the method, learn some times tables, and start to see how different numbers connect.

Have a little experiment on the page opposite.

I've popped a little frame up for you, you know, just to feel all arty…

Here hangeth the first original Colour Calculation by

....

When a number is multiplied by itself the answer is called a square number.

A trick to remember these square numbers is to see them as exactly that…**squares**!

To help remember what number is being multiplied by itself, you can paint a diamond next to it like this…

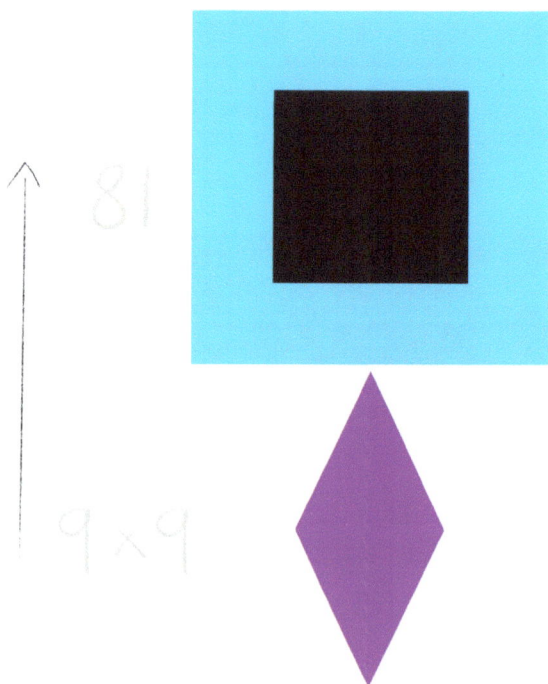

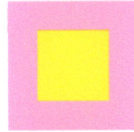

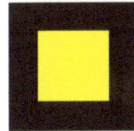

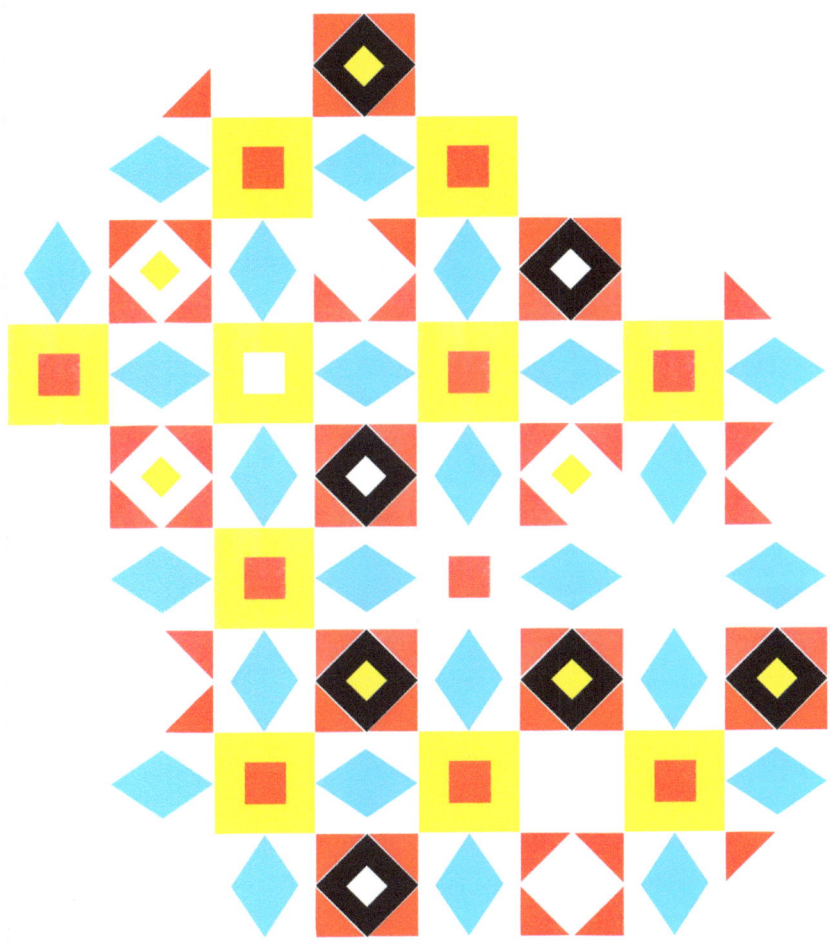

In St.Leonards-on-Sea, the town I was born and where Alan Turing grew up, there is a long alleyway called 'Bottle Alley'. Its walls are covered with millions of tiny bits of broken glass like a giant mosaic. Colour calculations don't always have to be neat and symmetrical.

They can EXPLODE across a page!

Have a go at adding to this mosaic and filling the page with as many calculations as you can…

Some Finer Details…

When showing a number with two of the same digits next to each other, for example 11, 44, or 377, I show each unit as though it is being held by the next unit. Try drawing some others...

This is a matter of design, much like how we each have our own handwriting style. You will find your own way of representing numbers. Just keep experimenting...

If a number contains two or more zeros next to each other, I draw a soft grey ring to separate the white.

That's pretty much everything, and what a *pretty* much it has been. But there's one last thing I want to show you…

One of the main things that made me scared of maths was the belief that I just wasn't clever enough to do it, a belief that got stronger every time I made a mistake.

But just as when making art, mistakes are incredibly important. In fact they can be some of our most important lessons.

So if you make a mistake in your colour calculation - do not give up! Recognise your mistake as an opportunity to make your work even *more* beautiful. Represent the mistake just as it is, a magical little moment… a learning curve!

years ago I moved to the city of Bristol with the plan of becoming a nurse. However, my plan didn't quite work because of one small problem...I failed the maths test.

Instead I tripped and stumbled into the world of art and somehow managed to paint and perform my way to a better understanding of myself, my past and my place in the world. Now painting is helping me understand this beautiful language of the universe, and I hope it can do the same for others, no matter their age or ability.

This journey of colour and discovery is only just beginning, and if there is anything it has taught me so far (beside from the times tables...!) it is that nothing, even a zebra, is just black and white...

Brook

Share your maths with the world…

@multicolourmaths
on Instagram

And keep up to date with new books and activities at

multicolourmaths.com